INVOCATIONS AND P~

Roger Ph
Dennis

CW00524459

Illustrations & Artwork by Roger Dennis
www.rogerdennisart.com

*W*ylde Publications – *Supporting the Wild*

ALL ABOUT ARTS
CREATIVE COLLABORATIONS

All About Arts & *Wylde Publications*

In Partnership: **All About Arts &** *Wylde Publications*
Invocations And Portraits
First published in the UK 2023.

All About Arts represents collaborative creativity in
all forms of artistic expression.

Wylde Publications is committed to publishing original
creative work in celebration of wild places and the wild within us.

Cover artwork & design and all pen-and-ink drawings
by Roger Dennis copyright © 2022.
Structure & Content Production organised by Steve Day
Photograph of Dennis & Day by Graeme Harris.
Printed & bound in the UK by Imprint Digital, Exeter.

*W*ylde Publications – *Supporting the Wild*

Dedications

Nicole Georgiana Townshend (1946 – 2020). (RPD)
Jennie Word-Witch, everywhichway. (SD)

INVOCATIONS AND PORTRAITS

"…there are so many great lines and images that are worth reading over and over. An internal authenticity."
Phil Madden (Wings Take Us, Paths, The Amphibious Place)

"I really admire the work... This book is such a luscious wonderful feast to read and thoroughly enjoy."
Pat Fleming (Thinking Like A Mountain)

Two Preludes

Day On Dennis

I met Roger when he began turning up at a series of concerts by the Day Evans Dale Ensemble – my poetry embedded within contemporary bespoke music. He then came to my more 'straight' readings. He'd bought my books, was clearly reading them; responded positively.

I knew who Roger Philip Dennis was – he'd won the National Poetry Competition in 2014 with *Corkscrew Hill Photo*, a mysterious 'portrait encounter' that demands the reader absolutely engages with it if they want to find its rich evolving resonances on human behaviour.

For me it's an exciting work, almost avant-garde in structure, yet at the same time deceptively matter-of-fact in its speech pattern. Despite his 'national' breakthrough, Roger has a low profile on the Devon poetry scene; better known as a successful incisive painter of both landscape and abstraction - as is immediately obvious from the artwork in this current collection.

Initially we tentatively swapped writings in twos and threes. Roger invited me for afternoon tea and the culinary wonder of his cake-baking after which our poetry sharing took on epic proportions. It became obvious to me that here was a writer of immense resources; dealing with 'self' and 'self knowledge', taking inspiration from that deep well found in Heaney's *North*, Sylvia Plath's *Bell Jar* and, perhaps strangely enough, the lodestone American, Robert Frost. Roger *is* the real thing; his visionary poem, *The New Taliesin* opens our collection; it literally is a breathtaking trip into his depth of vision.

To ground the concept of *Invocations* I'd also cite examples of his 'incident' poetry: *Pius Le Noir (Journey To The Interior)*, a story asking a multitude of questions from a variety of angles, seemingly on a hike through a foreign landscape, *Bed Legs* and *Absence*, two oblique poems about loss, both caught in moments of personal everyday experience. To borrow from Bob Dylan, these pieces speak truth *like ice, like fire.*

We decided to present our work together out of a common regard. Though our writing is different, perhaps extremely so, we felt a synergy between each other's intention, precision (or lack of it) and musicality. The two of us hold to the central tenet of reaching an understanding of humanity through examination of 'self'. White male poets, roughly the same age, living within the same radius, clearly having had extremely different lives now played out as friends; okay, we publish, with the proviso of Yeats tolling in our ears: *What then, what then*?

Dennis on Day

What I look for in poems is "Fizz". Yes, *fizz,* perhaps not a widespread technical term, but well describing the bone-tingling excitement I got from my first experience of Steve's music-and-word performance, from the quality of his music as well as that of his words, and also the conviction and animation of his stage-delivery. A conviction only reinforced when I turned to reading his work off the printed page, particularly (aside from this collection) in *Diamonds In Streams*.

Fizz. What gets under my skin, and manages to both surprise and feel familiar at the same time. I don't know why this is with Steve's work, as it is very different from mine. Steve has referred to this selection as "pairings," as it alternates Dennis-Day throughout, but I think of them more as juxtapositions that contrast yet nevertheless complement each other

Indeed, my first reaction when Steve sent me the draft of *Invocations and Portraits* was "What is this man doing, why has he put *this* with *that*?" For instance, the opening pairing, a straight forward low-key narrative of mine where the narrator is given a one-night stand on a plate but is unable afterwards to resist holding on too tight, is followed by a tender account of Steve's two old, if not ancient, citizens pictured in the decline of their days, which is not only tender but also picturesquely, if not grotesquely, rococo, in that the dozing couple are likened to scaly reptiles, garden gnomes, and shrew-eaters…

And yet, I get a resonance one from the other, from contrast as much as any similarity (maybe none!) that back-to-back the poems are both stronger, and if not more complete, then more extended, richer than separately.

Are Steve and I coming from the same place? — Wrong question, as the answer is either, "Obviously, yes," or alternatively, and just as appropriately, "No way!"

I have been happy to leave the choice of pairings to Steve, trusting in his musical sense, as his musicianship certainly exceeds mine. In his jazz-formed music, the wild leap from a theme to unexpected note(s) is uncontrovertibly the right one, and so in his poetry. Subject, image, and reference can take wild and rococo leaps that are equally incontrovertible; so in this collection, the leap from one poem to another is just, so it seems to me, music.

Contents

Afterword

Invocations – Overture

A New Taliesin (RPD)

You can find me in the picked
sweet flowers of the mountain
and the sweeter corn of the valley
hear me in arias of the opera
and the kicked can of the alley
I am a rumble in Metropolis
an ode to joy in Oceania
I have freed souls who walk in chains
then sold them out again
I have leapt ice flows in the North
danced with penguins in the South
I have been a drop of dew in the night
a speck of dust in a sun shaft
I am the bitter pip of knowledge
in the golden apples of the Sun
I am the pomegranate seeds
Persephone left untouched in Hades
I am the frayed hem of the skirt
trailed by the Queen of Night
the torn cuff of the coat Genghis Khan
left uncollected at the cleaners
I am the dancer in the dawn
the sleeper in the brightest noon
I was the moth that nibbled holes in Genesis
the woodworm in the truest cross
the first sea-wave to break on Atlantis
the first firework to sprout over Pompeii.
I have separated children from their mothers
and mothers from their senses
I have torn the fabric of society
and sewn it up with a live shock wire
my gestation was forty days
in the belly of the last Vestal Virgin
my death was forty days buried
in the concrete coffin of Chernobyl
I have hitched rides on Apollo missions
mined the moon for violet flavoured simples
twelve wise men have cursed me

with bell, book and candle
I have given sight to the blind
with an eye stolen from the Gorgon
twelve foolish virgins have blessed me
with rose water, aurum potabile, and babycham
I have played shape-change with the octopus
eaten soil with the mole and the worm
twelve brown-eyed bisexuals drowned on the Titanic
surfaced from the sea to crown me Taliesin the True
I was seaweed round the legs of King Canute
the sparrow that flew through Bede's mead hall
I am the rainbow that cuts the sky in half
I am the storm that shakes trees the way
an angry waiter shakes crumbs from a table cloth
my name is First of the Last and Last of the First
my name is known by the infant at the breast
my name is a closed puzzle to the universities
my name is a whisper at the edge of hearing
my name is not Taliesin in a looking glass world
where I put the finger I scorched oiling cogs
of Nimrod's construction engines to my mouth
and saw all the withered fruits of the earth
and the dark riders on their silicon-chip horses
I became liver-fluke, lamprey, the crumb of bread
Demeter brushes from the executives' table suite
and feeds to the chickens. Seven hundred years
I remained in the egg, incubated
by a rota of seven gold-feathered swans
thereby I know each and every swan song
and no word and no note is hidden from me
Taliesin is but the beginning of my name.

Sestina For Christina Langrish (SD)

Uzbekistan is the last place on earth you would travel
to find the woman round the corner, yet she lived there
teaching a curriculum so rich in detail, to expect to read
its cover on former Soviet soil is groundbreaking. Stoned
land inhabited by Sunnis living in a ditch of drumming.
Christina Langrish is a rare breed of English knowledge.

Percussion's ripple is extinct in England; like knowledge,
it remains ambient until unexamined maps of travelling
upset parliament - the rough skins of echo, rolling drums
for wars. In Uzbek animal hide is the peace scale of their
music. Even in the City of Tashkent a stove of hot stones
means a sophisticated meal of Noni Afgani. Turn and read

flatbread baking hieroglyphics in their manuscript, reading
the evening in lengths of moonlight. Christina's knowledge
has become a slippery spelling; ankle twists on uneven stone
slabs between Duckspond and the floodlit playing field travel
her feet down the garden path, tripping over what was there
to what could happen as she thunders like a roll of drums.

Buckfastleigh was a cotton-mill of *mind*fields and oil drums.
It inhabits Dartmoor like a comfortable well-read reading
shoe; a frayed-thumbed novel hiking steps from here to there
and back again. *The Valiant Soldier* contains the knowledge.
The Singing Kettle is where Christina discards a trail of travels,
cups a cup of tea, and from her sole removes the sharpest stone.

Christina Langrish is so much younger now, she tosses stones
like fireworks. She left her precious Uzbekistan home drumming
up a call to prayer, those tribal ties a maze of knots, travelled
back to a cider apple abbey where five days a week she read
the writing on the wall in broken English. Her deep knowledge
is now observed, silencing herself at Quakers' equator. There

on the edge of a circle of chairs, parch the bare bones of their
unseen Qur'an and Torah, known but unwritten. The old stone
meeting house where the window light splinters all knowledge.

In Christina's mind come Uzbek's Orchestra of flute and drums
playing midday dances, so she finds a Rumi love-poem to read:
Persia's perfumed pomegranates, not far for a heart to travel.

Uzbekistan, Tajikistan, Moscow; travelling to traverse where there
are crescents in the sun and people read their lives in piles of stones.
Christina still hearing drums, searching out their depth of knowledge.

Part One: Your Whispering In My Ear

You sat with a bunch of friends of a friend of mine (RPD)

You sat with a bunch of friends of a friend of mine
across the bar with a pint of heavy and those strands
of almost curling hair that didn't quite
hide how your eyes kept catching mine.
Then you said, No, you couldn't stay, you had this
farewell party to go to. But would I like to join you?

Your alarm went off at six a.m. but what woke me
was your whispering in my ear you'd really like
to get to know me more, spend morning by my side
as you rushed to catch the train to catch the ferry
to work your summer on the silver darlings.

And me, I was pen pushing, undoing
dot by careful Rotring dot the careless
or deliberate disposals in medieval middens
and while August bored its callous smile
right through the draughting room's one window pane
skewed nails, broken buckles, gap-toothed combs
dropped pilgrim badges and luck-leaked charms
monochromed my daily drawing board.

I walked down to the harbour pier hoping I could catch
in the tang of salt sea spray something of your scent
but all I got was iodine and the tarry choke of fag ends
that tracked the tourist trail.

"It's a bit tough," I wrote, "to find all my friends saying
'good-bye' at once. But thanks for the cards, they're great
and I hope at least the rain has stopped for you."

"I'm getting used," you replied, "to the rank reek
though I think I'll never get it from my nails —
the gloves they issue make fingers thumbs
docking pay, we're best without."

"It worries me," you said when at last we met
"that it seems to be meaning more to you

than to me." And I, I grinned
in attempt to give your words the lie
while anticipations and the head on my pint
frothed and spilled and slipped slowly to the floor.

Folk Song (SD)

The ol' folks, he's Moss Green,
carries stubble like a caterpillar
and she's bent double, twice grown
as the garden gnome she called boyfriend
when they were both as young as yesterday.
And they sing in the evening, the pure folksie
ballads, the ones with melodies that wheeze
harmonium and Smithsonian hardback hymnal.
They crack their wet-dipped tongues
on repetition. Vowels bubbling in the dim-lit fire,
smoking grey like the Vatican with a new pipe,
correction, Pope, and hope no one notices.
These ol' folks are reptiles, scaled with
the mathematics of aging, the letter *e*
is everywhere, in each epistle to the vipers,
swallowing whole shrews rather than eating them.

As I went out one morning
they were both asleep on the porch,
still open mouthed, propped up
in their wicker chairs.
He, snoring the barley mow laid to
harvest in his larynx.
As for the woman, like all women,
her sting had softened in sleep.
Breath came in little deaths that kept her
alive to the folk song playing on her lips.

Wistmans (RPD)

(Ordnance Survey SX6177)

I met Isabella de Fortibus coming through the wood
her silk gown green from moss and lichen hoar in her hair:

"Oh I am sick at heart and would lay me down and die
from trying to make count of all the trees growing in my wood!
Every time a tally's made, there's a baying of the hounds
with cries of 'Whisht!' to right and 'Whisht!' to left
and the Dark Man shrilling on his knife-sharp pipe
and in the darkness of his passing my mind is wiped slate-clean.

I wake on dawn's hillside with all my count to make
fearing that my trees are seedlings ripped up in the storm
High Willhays sends to scour his scarred and heathy moor
with his henchman Herne driving all before into Dart's cold arms
and oh I am soaked to the skin and oh so tired of life
from trying to take count of all the trees growing in the wood!

Yes I was Queen in Castle Carisbrooke and Lady of the Wight
Countess of Devon, and of Aumale, and Holder of the Honours
of Skipton, Holderness, and Brunswick, from Hampshire
and from Yorkshire my income came in pounds by the millions
I banked with Riccardi of Lucca, knew the Statutes of The Realm,
not Edward King of England, not Edmund Crouchbank, not
Simon de "Mighty" Montfort could lay a hand on me and mine
but all my wealth and power turns to Dartmoor mist
and oh! I am skin, and oh! I am bone
in the counting of the trees that grow in Wistmans Wood."

Local legend has it that Wistmans Wood, owned by Isabella, was also planted by her. However local lore is probably out by a count of thousands of years, as the wood is supposed by authoritative experts to be the remains of indigenous ancient woodland.

Six Claws On Ai Weiwei's Dragon Vase (SD)

There are six claws pictured on Ai Weiwei's dragon vase,
a near replica of the priceless porcelain Ming era original.
Emperors had only been permitted five claws; by imperial
decree the adding of additional claws was a capital offence.

A white marble Shakymuni sat beneath the Bodhi fig tree
solid as rock; maybe this is the unreliable truth of Twitter
or a genuine Qi Dynasty lotus Buddha. He is a silent sitter,
waiting in a carved mudra prayer position to free his body.

All the detailed evidence in this fine art exhibition flatters
the facts of revolt in exile, for the whole-wide-world matters.

Puzzling the iris and understanding is to ultimately ask why
the liberty of doubt is the best visual weapon we can hope for.

Ai Weiwei's six claw dragon offers permission to be unsure.
Oppression can only create the excuse to execute the eyes.

....

The beautiful narrow boat home on the River Cam is too small
to carry a Chinese conversation rocking the towpath mooring.
Sunlight sinks beneath Beijing, then rises in the trees shredding
the colours of quarter tones into the descant rippling of rainfall.

"So, art lovers, is this vase the fool-proof article?" asks Ai Weiwei.
He alludes not to a sixth claw but to the pitch on the grip of power.
We who wish for no borders have learnt to ignore the Babel Tower.
The reign of rain spits its sparks into his electric kiln of china clay.

We doubt the two headed dragon of Hong Kong will self-immolate.
Pearl River Delta's fireboats float flames upon the water in a state

of extinction while a rare red glaze of liberty colours the sixth claw
drawing the blood of scratched protest. Revolution, a Chinese urn

deliberately dropped by Ai Weiwei. An uncomfortable lesson to learn,
an act of prophetic symbolism promises only a pitcher, nothing more.

On Seeing A Performance of The Bacchae (RPD)

Dionysus came like a star from the East,
a star that sang.

The score unfolds:
discords, questions like razors: "Where behind Beast

do we find Human?
Is there birth in blood, construction from corpse?"

The old tales
had it so. And beneath Ecstasy, a purpose?

All our golden means
frenzied by Assyrian starlight, blasted by storm.

We synthesise
Judas-kissed Christs while our curtain songs form.

Dionysus came like a star from the East,
a star that sang.

Cohen's Cracks Of Light (SD)

......Forget your perfect offering,
there is a crack, a crack in everything,
that's how the light gets in.

Anthem – Leonard Cohen

In this glare of swelter-spots of illuminated
vision it is impossible to see Cohen's cracks of light.
For that I need the backdrop of the black bitumen's
lack of electricity and feel the sun curdle in my sight.

It is in the nature of slits sliced with blades
that have already cut flesh. Fresh air's chicken broth
of hunger with each emission saturating the breeze.
Your perfect offering of offal sacrificed on the altar

is a thing of the past, the sacred dead cow
burnt to a cinder of itself. And there in those cracks
of firelight are the peepholes into an everything that
allows for light to get in and out, for the blind to see.

Of course he groans medieval anthems of love's disease,
he was a poet prior to rehearsing his singer of sackcloth.

Invocation (RPD)

Come by earth and fire and water
come by wood and deep moonshine
come by mile and midnight measure
come by sinking ship and shark's sharp fin
come by king's fool son and captain's daughter
bring light to sun cloud-slaughtered
give twist of darkness no safe quarter
come by iron and tin and copper
by ruby, beryl, pearl and chalcedony
by saxophone and clarinet
tambour, trumpet, klaxon call
come by loud or not at all
save son of king by captain's daughter
save captain's daughter by wild swan call
bring light to sun cloud-slaughtered
come to those whose toil is tilling soil
to those whose toil is welding word
who set silence with a silver seal
beyond darkness and behind the sun
come by earth and fire and water
leave the dead to what they've done
bring life to sun cloud slaughtered
come by mile and midnight treasure
come by lake and cold moonshine
the captain, he's been scuttled
by his daughter on that island
where all touched turns to gold
his daughter, she's been made
Royal Poisoner to the King
so come by fast and come by slow
come by peat and come by coal
by oil, by tar, gasoline and methane
by fission, fusion, cosmic radiation
by natural gas and kerosene
the captain's daughter, she has learned
the pibroch pipes, the dulcimer
the glass harp, the electric mandolin
she's piped her father overboard
she's piped the king asleep

she's piped the prince a leaden hose
and flown on backs of thirty swans
shorn shadows from the moon
sung stories in the thickest wood
to bring life back to cloud-slain sun
to twist sad darkness from its shell
to set silence with a silver seal
so come by saxophone, come by flute
come by cymbal and the castanet
come by notes you cannot hear at all
come by earth and fire and water
come by steel and platinum
come by mile and midnight poison
by instinct, guess, or cobbled reason
by what the dead know behind their door
by what life measures on its ballroom floor
by song of megalith on sphagnum moor
by light of sun cloud-sloughed
come by blood of royal heir
by bullion from kings' vaults
by swan's down plucked by captain's daughter
come by cold fire, by dry water
by air that holds the earth in thrall
come by soon, or not at all.

Lingua Franca (SD)

(i)

I offered no response to a foreign language
other than a list of drummers in rhythmic
cycles beating elements of lingo.
I could not hear a reply to prayer or be there
for the proclaiming of the Second Coming.
What is spoken about in the light of day
is broken down by sleep seeping into
pieces of stone and clay erected out of
laity's Papal dreams, cradling them at night,
out of sight, out of mind as if icons
on the path to righteousness.
They are not;
this is a less travelled uneven way.
The sound of mantra, coda Creole,
Walcott's Caribbean through Homer's voyage
breaking the bow-wave
in a desire to come – home.
I used to write double Dutch and recite
all my responses in good faith.
That was then, now I recognise
the best dressed priest had been
a lapsed Catholic clothed in dharma.
Maybe Leonard Cohen undressing
for the public *songs from a room* in Greece.

(ii)

At Ugbrooke the ornithology is a pretence.
Pheasants are not the *Wild Swans of Coole*.
Game birds, fancy a plain bird for supper?
No, these creatures are resplendent
in iridescent surplices.
They take to tarmac, become grubby
road-kill peckings for magpies,
incantation squabbling for meat pie,
stretched beyond purpose, dead
already regurgitated and reincarnated into fly.
Such are today's cadenzas of chorus

sung sharp, excuses for a lack of belief.

(iii)

Lingo linguistics of Latin
massed into an indigenous litany
ushering in the coronet to continually
conquer a twist of pigeon English dialect.
Celt, Gaelic, Saxon, Roma, Conquistador,
in those capital letters comes
the typewriter tap of fan-dance spellings.

And in Roger The Rhymer's
incredible invocation I hear my own
fly buzzing into too-full ears, a kind
of fearless doubt caught up in
cockney tolling Bow Bells.
I cross the Rubicon River,
south of Battersea, down to China Town.
I-become-I–Ching's best bet, a head
to crown among Pearly Kings and Queens.

Sound of Sounds (RPD)

Stronger than the strongest swear words
"Ow!" "Ai-ee!" and the long
long lament palely writ "Alas!"

We have seen it floating in off the Moor
twilight, as the rooks caw out
their indecisive dance from roost to roost

We have held it in the open palm
of a hand we can make no gentler:
chick-fragile, the so-loud start of silence

if angels, the noise of foot-stamp
if devils, the lilt of prayer
if human, the thought before utterance

we have seen the sound hover
in bubbles the trout blew in the leat
in heaped soil piled by the mole

a one legged stand, a fulcrum
the world turns on, the sound
of the beginning.

At Laxton (SD)

The month of May plays tricks,
splits the stone Mary, grassed, stooped to a stop
knee deep in the watercolour of Hay Tor
a foot below the bed linen and fern already unfurled,
growing dense and wet with night showers.
By the high quilted hill with the ley-line crevice of
grafted coxes under the barrow rise of mid-summer
I am retired.

And sheltering beneath the Hound's lip as it
dips down two miles to the cattle-grid at Poundsgate,
are the early fruits of an old orchard.
Committed pickings, I gather their cores in my sleep,
incessant rain tapping rap upon the window.
I am sucked into the bay of body, pungent with the
scent of vixen married to cats and domesticated insects,
 my own turd tracks leading to an end of beaded neckline.

At Laxton I have come home.
The collecting of red berries, newt-life in the thick
slick of blanket weed, a day's netting of
clover and rare poppy seed. Cariad reading a map trail
across the Appalachians as I hang onto the
beat of Bodhran in my head rather than flicking wrist
and fingers at a drum. For I have come here to sound her.
Hear apples fall.

Traces (RPD)

Not noticeable at the time, just a few grains, barely a dusting.
Not so much taste as sensation of the tongue, as if walked on
by spiders, dry and sharp, sloe spiced with honey. You'd think
it'd be overpowered by the iron-sweet cloy of blood, but it lingers on.
Mistletoe pollen. Wind blown. Dust on cooling bread. Infusion
of mead. Or scattered from the wreath round my head. Food
they say, of the gods. As I, as we all. Before. Before the intrusive gift
of softness.

Before mud and sphagnum, softer than fleece, softer than the tufts
of bog-cotton waving over my head, softer than the damp velvet nostrils
of bulls, that grazing the heath, came to drink, and snorted, bellowed,
shied away from the necklace of blood at my throat, the axe-blow
baring brain to the stars. Before.

Before peat mire darker than un-milked tea, a vinegar Lethe, tanning
skin, reddening hair, embalming tissue, smoothing out the long slow
sink into the deeper dark. All the while the pee-wit! Pee-wit! Of curlew
the drab brown scurry of lark through myrtle and heather, the breeze
heavy with gorse blossom, with catkins of alder and willow, the clouds
drizzling sleet, snow, hail, the downpours of daylong drenching, day
on day, the brief sunlight, the lark scurries, the risings. The lark song.

Then one day, the peat-cutter's spade.
A water-blacked log, picked up, is thrown at the worker's mate.
Hits the ground. Splits. Out falls a human foot. The police.
The archeologists. The partially exposed re-interred. Then dug out
in one sarcophagus block. Stretchered to the hospital freezer.
Radiocarbon. CT, xeroradiography, atomic absorption spectroscopy.
Intrusions by scalpel and by lens. The soak in polyethylene glycol.
Frozen ice solid. Freeze dried. The display case.

Reflected in the boxing glass, goggling museum trawlers find
their eyes in sockets in my skewed face, their torsos in my
*"naked but for fox fur armband mid twenties one point
seven three meters sixty four kilograms well groomed
hair trimmed beard filed fingernails"* body turned leather sack.

But long ago I quit skin and bone. Moved into pale long leaves
tapered as farewell tears crossing a lover's cheek. Made my home
on apple tree or poplar, or even, that king of kings, the oak, a realm
not water, earth, or sky. Where song thrush feasting on my white berries
coats beak and claw with cling of waxy seed and so winged
and hymned I am translated godlike through sheer air.

That Western Ordnance Of Old Orient (SD)

That western ordnance of old Orient on yellowed paper
no leeway for latitude. Torn scratched scrolls that chart
cloven desert prints. Everywhere east of Albion falls apart
as the magi carry a storm of stars, always coming later.

Shock-and-awe, Seven Pillars of Folly to what men can do,
erected for a resurrected Orient to seal the fate of things.
After all, it was not the Virgin who visited the three kings,
they made the journey with funeral gifts for gentile and Jew.

The orientation of war founded by a holy apostolic church,
their weaponry scented in Myrrh and Frankincense, the stale
air of battlefield; Apache And Cobra, their hellfire laser trails
signaling the sky always-all-ways west of where we search.

See the Nighthunter, Orion Nebula, equatorial constellation,
a sighted survey of clusters caught in a depth of telescope,
mapped as a warrior defeated by neon in Big Bang's creation.

An immeasurable gap is patterned between Orient and Orion,
art to armoury, ordnance extending a sonnet written in hope.
Charmed snakes dance in the bazaar, offer scales to rely on.

The Salmon Lying in the Depths of Llyn Llifon (RPD)

The title is the first line of The Ancients of the World, by R. S. Thomas.

So full of knowing, of wisdom grown
she's long given go to going
holding stars for familiars
holding days in dallying eddies
poled immobile on her perched pendulence.

All the curious of the cosmos
career in hunt of her golden hazelnuts
that ever give grasping fingers slip.
Her one eye winks incandescent
setting glow all the pooly depths of Llyn Llifon.

Hibiscus (SD)

This summer is loaded into shower bursts of budding
hibiscus, a scattering of frail flower-heads hugging
torn mortar. Strange angels buzzing the slip-dipped
blur of wings. A fluttering of seizure and white tipped

stamen, flags striped chalky blue, pricked out of frost.
The plough-blade of stars laid upon the thick dross
of wasteland constantly tilled into rubble and thunder.
A turning over of salt stone, splitting tongues asunder

like mouths of Northern Archangels blowing petals
of hibiscus. See how the spring signings now settle
on these delicate stems of flora while talk of power

grows wilder. Nature ignores the arguments of metal
and men. The seeds of time count hours into hours,
as rooted detritus hibernates hibiscus into flower.

Dartmoor Dreaming (RPD)

Night pillows me between extremities.

North, the bleak wet playground of the Moor
loamy with fog and ancient history
its richest crop the bumper sprawl
of tourist cars, a rash of chrome
in prickly summer heat. Its season
is out of season.
                South
the dual carriageway's drone-and-whistle
throbs a splinter under the nail of sleep.
Its season is convenience.

I dream violence
a sudden severing of slip-roads
tyre scream, eel-twitch of tarmac
pumping tail-backs. Cities
dislocate, drift apart.

        Silence.

A clockless aeon later
out on the moor, in moonrise
thunder and rainstorm, a megalith
stirs, yawns, opens mica-shot
and bloody-hungry eyes, heaves
granite bulk inch by heathery
gorse and bracken inch
straight for town.

Elegy And Dirge (SD)

We could not carry what was left
of the carcass to its final resting place.
Unknowingly it had found finality
without the intervention of farmers
who are no longer shepherds
or artists who only landscape on flat canvas.

In the gully, the river bed a hollowing
pillow of moss and baked clay.
A cavity in the dry stone wall had tortured
the old ewe, eventually providing
rough death's refuge.
She had struggled and died,
no rest, no shelter, now dead sure enough.
There is little reason to move the sodden
fleece and bones.
The birds have tended to the eyes and flesh.
Strange how the skull now seems so small
and lacking in weight.
Nine months from now there will be no evidence
that a weak arthritic blackfaced sheep
came to grief at this graceless spot
of thorns and bracken.
We continue to follow the path
which has pilgrimed over these fells for centuries.

For the poet, Bridget Thomasin.

The God Deserts / Scent of a Vanishing Act (RPD)

Burnt cooking oil, acrid, plastic, mineral
limpets onto the back of his throat
as he leaves the bar by the kitchen entrance.

The other four stay drinking at his table.
One coughs, searching her Chardonnay
for the promised *'apples, with a flowery*

hint of lime'. The independent candidate
for the City Council leers up
from her evening newspaper, his face

almost honest through her wineglass base.
Strange, her olives, slightly singed... or is it
just those smoky bacon crisps? And then

the windows rattle in their jambs. An explosion.
Side street, contained, no civilian injuries. Nothing
left inside his car, though, but charred scraps.

Two blocks away a young woman
pushing a pram stops, scowls, swears
at the sudden noise that stirs the child.

The funeral goes by the book.
So many lilies! The woman
from the four in the bar sneezes

throws the rose, the forget-me-not posy, the
opera tickets, onto the coffin fair and square.
But even as the earth is spaded in

he's at the wheel. Rolls down the window.
Too much *Eau d'Hercule, parfum*
pour homme, her leaving present

complete with retro Thirties figurine
jingling from the ignition key. The Porsche
purrs off into the All American Night. Back

in Blighty, the girl (seeming much younger now
though maybe that's the make-up) rocks
young Anthony into a half-eye snooze

and sniffles into a g-and-t. Her hanky,
already damp, wafts Comfort, lavender,
Chanel Number Five, with just that hint

for old times sake, of patchouli.

Three Threads Of A Red Lacquered Trumpet (SD)

(i) Sonnet

Trumpet track, Take One: flamenco to fugue
across scrub desert terrain, sand blown down

the streets of San Diego like the sound of rain
bursting his name on blues riffs and rearranged
as *Spanish Key*. These are bruises Frances knew,
paid for in lacquered love; the lies turned true.

Playing the street-wire of desire so many times
his embouchure of a kiss is yet another split lip,
yet she endured the bountiful supply of voodoo
paid in advance (they knew Columbia would do.)

What is this thing? Sophisticated harmony lines
drawn across the wrists to get an ever larger hit.

Someday a Prince will come with a golden thread
tied so tight even his horn will turn a brighter red.

(ii) Horn Of Supply And Demand

This is a man
who eats his way to stardom.
Sups on supplies of chocolate,
trains his eye to Mars.
This is a man
wedded to a cornucopia
so short of universe the Red Planet
is twinned to the rim of Tunisia at night.

I heard him play trumpet, spitting salt through
the brass as if mining meaning
was the colour of the Cosmic Cliffs of Carina.
Closer to home, he consumed chapatis,
music to his mouth, medium paced
and very slightly toasted as if he were
Burning Spear at Montreux.

This is a man
clutching the tune of his wallet.
Firing accusations at the target
he erected for himself.
This is a man
blowing his demands and
supplements as continuous pleasure
until he sinks his soul in a vast sea of stars.

(iii) **The Golden Thread**

It does not seem so long ago that I first
heard Frances had let go of the golden thread
that connected her to the music emanating
from the red lacquered trumpet Miles Davis
pointed at the floor; each note squeezed into
a white plaster cast of her tiny footprints.

She had spoken softly in the wistful wordplay
observations of a morning sunrise while
finding his Harmon mute at the Blackhawk.
Her final melody-line, written in watercolour
pencils, described a slowly ebbing ending tide,
just as the higher register died beneath her feet.

The golden thread now lies cut in two, completed
by the first chorus, always destined to come last.

Corkscrew Hill Photo (RPD)

All afternoon she counts the sounds
until the fly-specked room crackles with silence.
Even the song thrush noteless. A thick drizzle
trickles rivulets down the window pane,
smears distance on fields, curtains-off hills
and greens the sagged thatch,
aches in the creaking gate and screws
watering eye to misting glass:
a hearse skids slowly up the muddy lane
blurs in droplets on a spider-web
spins sideways into darkness....

      ....rattling cough of cattle, rusty tractor,
      hinge of paint-peeled door, gears
      of cars forced to back in one-track lanes,
      buzz of pylons spanning the hum
      of outboards in the yachtsmen's creek,
      yelp of kids in the converted Mill
      the soft click-click of a camera-shutter
      up Corkscrew Hill....

The casement steams with sunset. She picks herself
up off the floor, mouth dry as mourner's grin.
Her arm reaches, shakes, reaches again
gathers the clattering jar from the shelf.
      "Cider?"
The landlord frowns, sniffing cat,
moth-ball, mould. She squares her back
on his fine view – the duck bob,
seagull clutter, gape of lime kiln.
      "And a nip of lovage,"
before he can point her
the off-licence hatch in the yard,
      "to keep out the damp!"
and smiles spittle.
Her flagon scrapes a scroll of varnish
the length of the bar's stripped pine
past bleating townies, past the regular's chair

and the corner where the photographer
sits draining her valley
through a tilted lens.

Mandala For Delhi   (SD)

There are so many sightings of India.
Mine was midnight
in Delhi
with a scrap of dogs foraging for rats
among the flapping piles of plastic under
a crumbling concrete bridge of poverty.

A caste untouchable takes a low
bow to the old town's bright lights
shining red henna on a curry full of sari.
The sludge of sewer-sex perforating
the night, a sperm count of millions
already passed, pissing subtraction.
Sacks of rupees and rice stored like
the poor on wooden platforms
impervious to the sight of another India.

I fear this hazy blind-spot, en route as I am
to an old figurine as thin as a Djinn
wrapped in a mandala of bribes for politics.
A boy barters a tin can of butane for a
rusting rickshaw advertising haircuts and
shavings, lettering peeling like snakeskin.
He punts for my black leather jacket,
telling me I wear the holy hide of the
scraggy dun cow tottering lame and soiled,
dragging its own dung like a placenta.

I had come to visit the Jains in the north
but remained here awhile, wiping bare feet,
measuring myself in a length of raga.
It's totally off the scale.

Dedicated to the poet/scholar Shrimad Rajchanda (1867 -1901)

Death of a Man of Words   (RPD)

i.m. L.P.D. 1910—1983

It was with great dif- *(variant spelling of dis-,*
assimilated before f ,) -ficulty *(facultas,*

'ability, opportunity,') we turned the still warm
so dead a weight body over.

I shut the eyes, but the mouth hung
reassuringly so much someone else open

raided, cleaned out of words, first victims
of the chaotic victorious invading cells, messengers

of the who-knows-if angels that had reached out
languorous delicate cotton wool arms to draw him

word by word to the write hand of god the lexicographer
who divides usage from abusage, script from scribble

the goofs from the ship-shape footnoted commentated
appendicised parenthesised annotated referenced

cross-referenced subscripted superscripted supplemented
with marginalia and addenda and all the glorious company

of saints Patter, Partridge, Roget, Brewer, Chambers, tenored
in Bach choir choral with the counterpoint

of ultimate punctuation.

We turned.

The face now a cast, a crossword without clues
a sleuthless whodunit, a dust-jacket

bookless.

Test/Edit/Test (SD)

That morning in June 2022,
when I tested positive for Covid,
I spent the aftermath rifling through
Roger's invocations, preparing a book
I will only half write.
And in the fog of phlegm
and cough linctus, read
his firing squad orders *in-memoriam*.
How a man of Pax, paint and
hermit kindness can bleed
like the rest of us. Dip his pen in the chronic
sentencing so close to the liquid of my lungs.
I too become his man of words caught spewing
self into the toilet basin.

Progress (RPD)

1

You come lightfoot with the morning mists
while I am still heavy and slow with sleep.
I go and fumble for a coffee.
There is dew and a leaf on your hair.

* * * *

Your breathing is ragged.
There are wrinkles round your eyes.
Your mind moves like the sun on waters,
your speech is music.

* * * *

A slipped slither of the moon
is your smile.
Your shapeless embrace
the sun's hollow.

* * * *

2

You have your hair dyed black,
your dress is grey.
A funeral passes by.
Perhaps, there are tears in your eye.

* * * *

Cold chips in your pocket
and grease under your nails:
your words are slow and heavy
but your feet laugh.

* * * *

(37)

You have watched the barges on the river
where the grass is sparse and black.
Your hands are empty
while meaning brims in your eyes like honey.

The Mouth Of The River (SD)

She is the eddy of the tides at the mouth
of the river, where whirlpools split south
to the Atlantic and due north to forever,
her poetry speaks a spell of fine weather.

Lexicon of waves spilling currents to fit us
into the *other* accents. A diamond litmus
test that cuts up the Looe into two stirring
seas and Polperro into old Welsh wording.

Her classic-naked-organic history of skin,
a covering. Dust-jacket warmth in the wind;
pages of leaves, charts of heart's prophecy.

She is above-ground, medieval as mined tin,
post-modern as registrar's ink minted deeply
beside a mouth of dried seaweed and algae.

First Estuary Encounter (RPD)

Paddington, Reading, Newbury, Westbury, Castle Carey, Taunton
     Exeter St Davids.
At noon the train came to a beach, grey, long,
     late November still
intimate with mist and mud-colloquial, lumped
     with loitering cormorant, dotted with gull
stabbed by dunlin and the thin bent needles
     of curlew, of avocet.
And slowed. For a moment
     I thought we travelled on water.
A wash of mist brushed blue haze
     over mute ochres of dead grass, over
the throat-lozenge pink of damp Devon sand
     pointillist with birds' blue foot-prints.
The water no colour at all
     a glass on vacancy.
The train's pace timed to ripples of windless tide.
     Passengers sighed, buried back
into books, walkmans, plastic coffees, shifted feet,
     avoided shared glances.
I almost hoped
     we would not move at all.
Sail-less yachts, anchored dingies, locked
     into their reflections
changed directions one to the other in neat ballet,
     in precise counterpoint
to our estuary edge continuo, a score
     re-writing the Music of the Spheres
— until a gin-trap station
     snapped a black mouth
down on the train. Dawlish. A lamp-post
     peered through the window.
No one got in, no one got out, all sat tight
     in private travellings
but when I turned back from the glass
     all my journey had changed.

The Bowler Hatted Surrealist (SD)

René Magritte tipped his thinning head of hair
to a row of ash lining the rim of the gorge,
lowered his hat brim to hide
those wide eyes from the sun.
He came to landscape the moor,
sowing seed in a sawn-off corner
of scrubland outside Brussels,
outside everywhere.
In his ever enthusiastic detail the great
picador of paint left the Devon window
overexposed so the sky turned to pink
cloud allowing the Blue Elvin rock face
to be wrapped in sheets of silhouette.

The small call from the river below
is the solo sound of a weasel
caught by a tortoiseshell cat.
We continue smooching to
the Lord's Prayer, lost in love
to do no evil, kissing non-closure
on Mahalia Jackson's *Amen*.

What we see in a tree-line
is a written composition,
the hat without a head,
a very different proposition
to the head that has no hat.

Midnight Chivalry (RPD)

On the first rung of the spiral stair
the monk leans, holding a candle,
listening to the stone-funnelled echoes
of Lancelot's heavy tip-toe,
of Guinevere's silver slipper
on the crisp midnight marble
of the tallest tower of Camelot.

To the monk's right, through the arrow-slit
the moon throws a blue-grey shadow.
From his left hand the candle casts
a sandstone shadow, bruise-brown.
He leans and listens. The candle tilts.
Hot wax scorches his fingers.
In the region behind his heart
in double gloom the shadows overlap.
He kneels to pray. Frost from the stone
skewers his knees, sharp as misericordes.

In the solar off the main hall
Arthur, beneath the imperial fleece
dreams of bonfire. And shivers.

Luther's Love Letter Of Indulgences (SD)

On Wittenberg's door is written the fatal flaw,
that scrap of indulgent parchment listing more
guilt and enmity than absolution can set free.
Nailed to the decayed bark of Old Eden's tree

is Luther's love letter scribing Wrath and Justice.
Believe it to be so, a handwritten parole. Trust it
as if this is the Holy Gospel According to a Snake
shedding scales of skin burnt raw on the stake.

Eve served China Chai straight into pottery mugs,
flakes of imperial dynasty, pulling the oriental rug
from under Adam's carved tray that carried them.

These guests are predestined to spill the odd jug
of milk over their diet of worms. Reptilian men,
waving a Bible they faithfully pretend to defend.

Part Three: Our Boat Rides Out

Salvage (RPD)

Our hopes shrink to dark matter.

Once helium-buoyant, full of harvest
fields sown, roofs raised, ovens fired.

Now too heavy a ballast to ride out storm.

To be jettisoned, to end up on come-what-may
shores, to disintegrate slowly, one more school
of beached whale in the tide-line plastics.

But then, freak chance, our boat rides out
hurricane, maelstrom, doldrum, only
to founder, scuttled, beneath your cliffs.

Salvaging, you discover in the hold

bodies packed in salt, laid out and composed
as medieval saints whose papery fingers
breeze stirred, gesticulate in Byzantine

and bewildering benedictions
confounding more than they absolve.

Djembi (SD)

I put the kettle-drum on
the stove to boil a roll,
learn to play the biscuit tin
for bourbons; 'tis the drummer
not the drum. My other eyes
are kept semi-shut for safe keeping
but I, the self, we are part of the
nomadic tribe of Nobodi - bought off
with a pair of bongos because
our feet tread lightly.

My first djembi came from Lagos.
I fingered the fur rim and it rang like bells.
Ibrahim Sangjany traded Nigeria with me,
held my hands and showed me how to paint
speech patterns into the scraped skin of a dry
milk-cow – exchanged at market, processed
and beaten into leather. Swiftly like migrating
swallows we danced Essex into Afrika and back
again, scatting spirit spray of rhythm across
the continental drift with bloodbeat intuition.

Decades later my drum tradition was finally
forged in Mozambique, crossing thunderclaps
with musicians who had all the timing in the world
except that their own country could not afford any
time for them. I-and-I wide open, eyeing their ears
to the well worn road of rusting foreign tanks left
like giant can-pans beaten with sharp machetes.
It was a hard week's work; djembi's hit parade, my
only strong arm, sunburnt inside a plain white shirt.

Back in Bristol came a meeting with a one-handed
drummer from Rwanda, asked to reconcile with the
man who had taken her left hand to the fire

and raped her 82 year old mother.
Oh djembi, beat a route to all name-changed
nations, curl my fingers and thumbs on drums
singing of Eswatini.

Dedicated to the memory of Honorine Mugabo

Bed Legs (RPD)

You know," she said, "you really shouldn't,"
rheumatic finger wagging, eyes bulged green and watery
as frogs about to leap the pool of her glasses, the tang
of cigarette browning her brown cardigan, "You really
shouldn't have," closing the tall repro Jacobean cupboard
on its dark waft of sherry, nutmeg and sesame salt
while my glance skeltered up the barley-sugar legs
of the oval table where I, smaller, not so very many
years ago had sat Wednesdays four o'clock for bone
china plates of iced-mice cakes and white traced
tractors, teddies, cows, on pink, green, and bisto-brown
sugar-iced biscuits licked more than they were bit
and the marvel of edible paper peeled from the base
of macaroons while the black lacquer wireless creaked
warming up its valves for the evening's Letter From
America and The Shipping Forecast when the green
glass crenellated ashtray would be well primed beside
the French novel summoned from patient storage
in the glazed teak bookcase sporting potted cyclamen
three more already flowering on top of the bureau where
she'd shown me the secret drawer-behind-the-drawer
that popped out when ("Eyes closed now!") the right spot
was pressed, but was disappointingly devoid of treasure
except for one dead fly and a broken cigar cutter. Only
the last time I'd asked to see The Secret Drawer
she'd stared blankly: "What drawer, dear?"

"You know," you repeated, "You really shouldn't have
sawn them off!" " Sawn off what?" " Sawn the legs off
your bed, it was a good one, the pair to my own."
Not long before, your daughter had taken to marking
each day's level on your bottle of white *Bin 33*
after you complained of dizziness and the room revolving.
So then I took you through to my room, showed you the bed,
its intact full-length legs. "Must just have been a bad dream,"
I said. But that was only partly reassuring. As if

you'd heard That sort of thing from The Young before.
When we found you sprawled out between the green
formica table and the gingham curtains we knew things
had really got critical. Meaning, A Home. The other side
of the country. My uncle's territory. We visited. You occupied
your own climate. One of fog. In brief bursts of sunshine
you knew my name, but not me. Though sometimes
as if a breeze lifted layers of dust sheets, you seemed
to catch the echo of some hidden drawer rattling
with broken cigar cutters, cyclamen corms
and sawn-off bed legs.

Stanley And Patricia (SD)

Stanley was a painter not a percussionist
and did not wish to be reminded
of the exact amount of rhythms beneath her skin
or the many times the drum-head gets tightened
to make it ring.
He was a man who visualised in oil
and paid a high price to fling a leg of mutton onto canvas.

Stanley smelt the turpentine as he ran his fingers through
his white fringe and loaded a brush with stretch marks.
She had tried to palm off her portrait as an affectation,
his life-class in every groped grin he threw in her way.
In the dimming dusk of each measured day
he pretended to pray
just as the swans came floating down the Thames
their heads tucked underneath their wings.

Stanley Spencer (1891 – 1959) and Patricia Preece (1894 – 1966)

Three Voices (RPD)

It was the sea
first told me
(slate blue the musseled
low-tide rocks
long fingers stretching into
breaker-froth)
What keeps you warm
in Winter
keeps you cool in Summer.

It was my blood
first told me
(moss-soft the rippled
sleep-washed limbs
light fingers curled on
pillow-lace)
What's best served warm
in Winter
is best cooled down in Summer.

It was the wine
first told me
(damson red the lipsticked
half-drunk glass
chewed fingers fumbling for
sleeping-pills)
What made you warm
in Winter
turns you cold in Summer.

Bookkeeping (SD)

A 1959 hardback edition,
drowned in a lap of books.
A written reef of shelving, stacked
in ordered notation, wave upon wave
of literature silent with grave meaning.
Grove Press, New York, the covering fly
sheet is a black-on-white tree of bones.
Bertolt Brecht's *Selected Poems*,
each page pressed into service
and stuck together by decades; a lack of
leafing, an ache in the age of bookkeeping.

I took it down and carefully pressed
the pages apart. Elaine said Michael
would have been pleased to think
she'd given it to me.
My eyes followed the lines of German
about a drowned girl gradually becoming
carrion over four verses beneath an opal sun.

There, pasted on the inside cover,
is the County Library label
of the West Riding of Yorkshire,
the creased colour of jaundice.
Could be a faded ration card that never
found any mouths to feed.
On the opposite page, dated Clitheroe 1982,
some official has scrawled in pale blue nib-ink,
Saved from incineration. They must have had clout
because it was tucked up for eternity
on Michael's book shelf in close proximity
to de Beauvoir, Brendan Behan and Beckett.

An irony, that drowned girl,
Ertrunkenen Mädchen,
decomposed so quickly

yet here she is, floating through
Brecht's pen, un-incinerated,
still a presence on the page.

Bertolt Brecht (1898 – 1956)

Dartmoor Metaphysics (RPD)

The architecture of Dartmoor is characterised
by "the dominance of the solid over the void,"
according to a National Park's publication.

the weight the emptiness the raw damp of it

the cold the paths petering out at dusk
sudden fog driving rain treacherous mire

the mines leaking arsenic to the leat
fly-buzz in the sweat of bracken

liver-fluke and tics in the sheep
the void in you

forget tourist romps over tors
no abseiling gets you out of this

lost in a fissure of granite
a blown egg beneath the logan

east west up down it's all one
solid everywhere and everywhere the void.

House Burnt Down (SD)

Caravaggio's running wounds were
eventually doused by liquid flame.
A familiar story if it were not for
his borrowed name, living as he did,
alone up there, painting a bonny under
the eaves of the elemental.
No one feeds or leaves without brimstone.

Up on the moor, where the path breaks
bones under the feet and
the blacken bracken is bedded down
beneath split timbers still splintering
tinder dust, it is the rain-rust pools
that host the hollow oak, roots and all.
At the time the cinders would have risen
into a sticky mix of scorched stars
over the shroud of nightsky.

Such a pathetic sight, the pyre of a man,
acrid air heating the heavens.
His thick grip of matted horse-hair turned
loose like a stiff mane and tail.
Then came the Johnny Constables,
beating the bounds of a house burnt down.
Tramping through bottles, squashed tubes
of colour fix, empty Calor Gas and candlewax,
a shattered sight to end the finer art of living.

Pius Le Noir (Journey To The Interior) (RPD)

For eight months the mountains threatened us with their blueness
while we got used to sun, sand-itch and a diet of dates.
Then a guide was found, small, leathery, smelling
of goat-lard and urine. His eyes side-stepped you as he spoke.

Weeks later, we made the pebble scree above the tree line.
Later still, we found the first blade, broken. And then
the hilt. And then a dagger, glinting among the stones.
And the wind. Leaning into it, hugging the gradient
we climbed slowly, slipping on pebbles, wind-whip tears
stinging chapped cheeks, the ceaseless off-key whistle
                                          in our beards,
blearily cautious of cutting our feet on the sharp blades
that now covered the ground thicker and thicker
notched, cracked, pitted, stained, bent, snapped, but none
beyond doing damage.

                  Then we all caught sight of it
at the same time: the hut on the skyline, wood and stone
towering barred and slit-windowed, piebald with moss and lichens
its leeward side black with fungi. "Who – lives – there?"
we shouted into the wind. Our guide leered, eyes crab-waltzing,
fingers itchy on his belt, "The Princess!" his words
hanging and hissing in the gale cool as hawks, "Gentlemen,
the Princess! Shall I,"– tugging at our sleeves " – announce
your arrival to her?" We stared at each other, and at
the spread of blades piling ever thicker towards the hut
but saw only the lowering crest of the mountain rising
curved and cairn-nippled, each man motionless dreaming
silk sheer and flesh-cool against his raw wind-torn face.

Until a crow rose cawing from the hut flapping rank
huge maggoty wings inches from our faces and we were
running, falling, groping, on up the mountain past the hut
into sudden deep snow-drifts. Our guide griping
and grizzling behind us. As we cleared the ridge
we caught a dazzle of gold in the sunset, turrets and domes

on walls of violet shadow piled on violet shadow. Our guide
fell prostrate on the ground, crying *"Pius le Noir! Principe
de los demonios! Pio il Nero!"* through mouthfuls of snow
and would not move, for all our kicking and promises
of gold, goats, honey and ermines. With night falling
we rigged him a stretcher from tent poles and canvas
and stumbled on downhill to shelter.

Paula Rego (SD)

*"I start to tell a story, but then as I tell it,
it turns into something else." Dame Paula Rego*

I start to tell a story about how
her pictures grit a mess of love
mixed with backstreet bacteria cut into
flesh, blood and forced labour but she
scratches a scream on brass plate,
fingernail blade subverting rivers of scarlet ink.

There is a cave in the belly for chromosomes
to live like stag beetle larvae; empty quarter
in which dream has no headway.
Suck out the opera of Carmen,
drop aria into a pail to compost apricots
purple and green; low hanging fruit picked
during the beehive's arrival in Portugal
from a land now known as Hungary.

The drive wheel in the printing press
has orbited its full circle
throughout the night.
By dawn a three-legged cedar tree table
holds a hundred twelve paged books;
each bear the signature *Paula Rego*,
written out as art.

They will journey by cart
pulled by mules and men
to the walled city of Lisbon.
Only the number of legs required to complete
a journey through such a terrain differentiates
these bedfellows, other aspects of behaviour
are identical.
God knows, all tomes of experience
must be treated as carefully as any infancy.
It is hard holding hurt and hellfire in
illustrated stories but living is drawn to
the pain of breath.

Grief Heatwave (RPD)

In the garden
no rain falls.

Beyond the gate
downpour rages.

The radio crackles.

"...Low pressure
over the Atlantic....."

In the house
dust motes dance.

A beetle-husk
spins on its back.

"....Widespread inundation
severe loss to farm stock..."

The photo-portrait on the desk
curls up on itself.

Thrushes smuggle snails
across the hedge

singing only at night
outside every window

on ladders of moonlight.

Always a river
the same river

poised
over the house

waiting its moment
of dam burst and gate break.

Moonstone (SD)

In a hand of spades,
a number of people gave up on me.
For sure, others bridged their hearts
as if the curious jester had suddenly
become a serious prospector of agate.
It is not the having of the hand
but how it is played among those who possess
no fingers and thumbs, no rings of precious metal,
that will eventually strike
moonstone in the mineshaft.

I found translucent stone, chipped out of
a glint of moonlit maths panned
in grains of sand running between a pack of cards.
It became this agate I give to you,
everything I ever knew
about the Queen of Clubs.
Breaking cover allows good fortune,
exposes the shuffled fingering
that produces a ringed deuce called devotion.

Border Troubles (RPD)

First signs –
            the delphiniums.
We were kept awake all night by the noise.

At first we thought it was wind in the trees
but it was a still moonless night
without a breath of air.

Later above the tinkling of hoses and sprinkler sprays
an unmistakable croaking from the roses.

Great-Aunt Edith
was convinced they'd been raised wrong
thorns all askew or petals too tight.

Tea-time, we pushed her out in her wheel chair
to give Rosa Mundi and Duchesse d'Angouleme
close inspection with spy-glass and magnifying lens

revealing what appeared to be rust was in fact
an infestation of minute but virulent red squirrel.

Soon she discovered the salvia was playing host
to a troop of thumb-sized blue baboon
adept at filching the cucumber out of her sandwiches
until we stood the legs of her tea-trolley in paraffin.

The last straw was the hyena in the hydrangea
precipitating Aunt Edith into lengthy and not entirely
amicable negotiations
with the local safari park.

An Encounter (SD)

For the Poet, Graham Burchell
& the Painter, Stanley Spencer

She sold me a beehive and
gave me the whole world.
At the time I had no hunger for
the sweet tang of honey nor did I
wish to travel any further than fifty miles
from the front door of the little house
I had negotiated with my leftovers;
kept my living interest on ice.

Yes, I saw her smiling, how
could I not? She took the elegant way
to the moorland microphone to perform
Burchell's *Up* without wearing walking
boots, instead her delicate black buckled
heels clicked like Ginger Rogers.
I turned tail to the little house and
read a swarm in the beehive book.

In the Train to Sarajevo is an
imagined moment in 1922;
a description of Stanley Spencer in
the act of art as an encounter.
Burchell writes like a fly on the wall
and I wonder if from his place in the stars,
had he seen me observe those
black buckled shoes walking *Up*
to the microphone as if on ice?

Part Four: Thunderous Glass Skies

Guilhem at Pentecost (RPD)

The desert has me by the throat.

In my three-cypress-shaded cell
beneath the mountain, I, panting
like a frog in the dark of a well
croak my Lenten litanies

at evening to Heaven's Queen
to the Son in the morning.

At noon, all tongues are fire.

Saint William of Gellone (755-812/4,) known in Languedoc as Guilhem, was a cousin of the Emperor Charlemagne, Duke of Toulouse, and a general in campaigns against the Basque Gascons and the Umayyad Emirate of Cordova. The medieval 'chansons de geste,' epic poems typified by The Song of Roland, *credit him with many colourful exploits such as the capture of Orange. In 804 he founded the Benedictine Abbey of Gellone, now called St-Guilhem-le-Desert, near Lodeve, and later lived there as a monk for the last six or so years of his life.*

Charlemagne's Menagerie (SD)

Charlemagne's exotic imprisonment
of minerals, botanical slaves, plants
pruned to the height of the thunderous glass
skies above his memento menagerie
of men and women caught in a captured calling.
Such is the wild flamboyant portable jailing
of wildebeest, zebra, young gazelles, chattering
striped monkeys and clipped-winged parakeets.
An arboretum trailed across Europe
in a caravan of forestry erected as if each leaf
and branch were sentries to a palace of power.

Into this warrior's playground of earthly
delights is paraded Abul-Abbas,
the great bull elephant of Asia.
Here is the ego of Empire.
Charlemagne owned the known world
and we perpetuate his decadence;
the white elephant in our zoo-menageries
where we tame the origin of the species.

I Asked the Ants (RPD)

We intend to take over the world
the day after tomorrow. We will start
in a small way, we specialise
in small ways.

We will sit up late at night
listening to the wind in the trees,
we will sit up late at night
studying the changing light of the moon.

We will collect many small black aphids
and transport them ahead in the vanguard
to establish a substantial reserve of supplies
and also to act as a buffer
between us and our unreliable allies
manoeuvring in from the forest.

We will store fermented aphid dew
in many multiple-bodied receptacles
for many a six-legged toast to our healths
late into the night, late into the night,
listening to the wind that will have turned
to torrents of rain pattering on the leaves.
We will take over the world
the day after the day after tomorrow.

We will sit up late at night counting the stars
careful to calculate the exact number
crucial to our campaign, operating
a Paracelsian procedure of *Particulars*
involving a solution of formic acid
and a *Prima Materia* of aphid husks.

We will sit up late at night listening to the tall tales
the windy moon whispers in the sycamore trees,
we will count the number of smallest possible ways
assigning to each of us a particular star.

(66)

We will wait through night's long *Nigreda*
through the *Albedo* of starlight
through the fluctuating *Citrinatas* of the moon
and then we will set off on our long march
all of us in a line of our small ways
on our small legs with our small sugars
and our small kegs of *Aurum Potabile*
the day after the day after the day after tomorrow.

Two Portraits In Repose (SD)

She spills her laughter and song
like throwing a lifetime to the wind giving it to me.
Summer in this address of apples stowed away in newspaper.
And today the sundress slips on her shoulders
and I relax into the ripple effect dancing
through her scrabble for harmony.
Scat and opera, the Welsh language of past Polperro
bubbling up in the comedy of my errors.
Take each other for what we are, celebrating the soundings
of the purring morning breathing *Myfanwy*.

I listen to her humming the clarinet
that has not left its case for a week or more despite
the desire to keep the reed warbler company. Instead she had
quietly written about *Ravens*, soared their wings
across wasteland. Clarity in a song that
will never have a melody or
find a way to Cardiff Bay in search of Shirley Bassey.
She can do better than that, her song and
dance are our privacy. Her poetry a declaration of colourings
outside my lines, a bard beyond two portraits.

Fog (RPD)

Eases in over the sea
like cotton wool on speed or the swing
of an eraser on the end of a very, very long pencil

embracing everything
with a mother-of-the-universe welcome
like the society hostess at the celebrity New Year party

the way she drains colour
the way she replaces everything *ex nihilo* and *intacta*
the way she reliably returns silently, unexpectedly, unasked for.

Or how she with close to no
warning removes all those busy toys — buildings,
cars, crowded beaches — from over-active sun, reprimanding

us all with her calm grey
blanket. Like sleep. Even when the world
re-emerges cautiously beaming its affidavits of good behaviour,

there remains the unshakeable suspicion
that new additions have been implanted unawares,
that familiarity's nest has been cuckooed by her cool eraser.

Tambourine (SD)

Half a moon is a night surge tide
planing a shaving of surfed sand
as it drags the jingle of shingle
out into a slew of sea.
I have never liked the tambourine.
Cheap tiny tingling tin
that rids a beach of music.
The exchange of currency,
a shaken clap of midnight's return
and the hand of a robber
always slightly behind the beat.
Half a moon carved out of the dark,
crescent lit in an angle of orbit.

I took up the tambourine
for want of a drum to harmonise
this seizure of surfing's parody;
another act of faith difficult to deliver.
Monk's *Trinkle Tinkle*, no siren of ocean.

Neither marine maritime nor shaken
tambourine contains any rhythmic clout.
Hit out, a wavering motion of jive rubbing up
against the slide of tides crumbling defences
back down to the depths of dissonance.
Waves crash cymbal into the coast.

My blood count rudiments strike empty air,
somewhere between half a moon and me.

The Tax Collector Lunches Alfresco (RPD)

Noon.

The road sizzles.
Sun glare spins orange fireballs.
Wind whips grit.

The fountain a trickle.

Orange trees
are shade enough
for a one-armed soldier
mount, dog, & fleas.

Petals fall. Lizards flicker. Ants
scurry. Sap bleeds
through sun-cracked bark.

Air thick with cypress, horse sweat
rosemary, thyme, dog pant, urine
garlic sausage, ripe goat's cheese.

A dropped fig splits, rolls
trailing bruised juicy pulp
across sun-scorched earth
to a marmalade

set with skin thin
as memories

that he weaves
into his to-be
tapestry of success.

He peels back each
blistered crusty layer
to the tender pink.

A noise of hooves on the road
limping clip-clop-clop of a nag
sulky plod of mule

the riders shading eyes against a sun
spinning even through closed eyelids
a windmill of orange fireballs.

¡Madre de dios! How many
dog days, how many hot noons
how many orange-ripening winters
must I labour in their pursuit?

Fabricated Yarns (SD)

(i) The Garment

Their home is a wefan studio of threads
where she has pogued poetry into
her sleeve of leaves and rolled up her silver
cuffs with earthenware.

She sat spinning stories, needling their
meaning, her breath a lisp of litany
of fine art wools made precious because
each sentence comes faceted
with spindle and safety pins.
She spins sophistication.

Describe to me spirals wound around sail knots.
Explain to me the meaning of America.
Tell me what it is to work with the tints of fibre
and feel them grow inside tissue.
Let all four of us compare ourselves
to moss rolled from stones turned mystique;
a maze of youth led astray into a fabricated age
where the length of our dyed lives
catalogues the nature of things.

I used to darn my own verse, tie it so tight
there was no light in its readings.
Now, I find warp and weft closer to the cloth,
daylight in the fingered seam stitched like thin
pale grains of English maple.
Woven bark marking the gaping sentencing
at the end of theology.

There is a Hokusai wave beyond the mussel sand,
a shot of stars above the tide, there is a
universe as dark as threaded strings of ebony
cotton cut-up over the Hawking holes of time.
In a corner of their ivory room

a woman carries a Chinese origami paper
fan gently stroking heated air
across this wooden bed of nails.

(ii) **Loose Ends**

And sew, threading a friendship through a row
of loopholes, catching each seam,
making the idea of a functional shirt surplus to
requirements. Gold leaf a belief in ritual,
take pleasure in poetic calligraphy,
the curve of a word rising out of woollen cloth
as if it were stiff parchment.
All stories are sewn into an orthodoxy
that becomes epiphany.
Such complexities of the simple life are found
in carefully ironed loose ends.
By all means make a promise but make it well.
Make it better. Better than the best man,
more beautiful than the nurse who baths
her own wounds; she kisses his lapel label,
in so doing ties his open necked shirt.

For Sophia & Tony Roberts.

Absence (RPD)

I went walking my local wilderness
past the ice-cream van and dozing cars
past paths way-marked yellow
up slopes sharp with ling and furze
where absence is a sunless medium
skyless as the rain-loaded distance.

I thought a booted stride would strike
harmonies, earth rhythms, nature notes
but no cuckoo called, no lark
surfed the sea of stonechat clatter.
Only croak of raven, only squelch
of sphagnum bog. And the wind's thin stutter.

I must have passed stone circles widdershins
whistled in megalith rows, for when fog
hid the hill my map too was wiped
slate clean, mist featureless, the air
clearing only for snatched glimpse
of sudden castles on intimidating hills
storm-brew silent but for crow parliament
and a half-caught baying I took for
the chant absence pipes in memory's
soft tympanum. Until

a pack of hounds cleared the brow
white-backed each with one red ear
and harried me uphill snapping
at my heels. Stumbling, I felt hot
breath at my neck, teeth at my throat.

I woke in my home bed. Beside me
the dent in the mattress still warm.
In the street cars blared musak. At the door
my boots still wet, peat stained. On the table
a crystal flask with a broken seal
and on the chair a dress of green satin

gold thread, amethyst, pearls, glittered
in a momentary sunbeam and melted
like moorland mist.

Boudhanath (SD)

When I stood in Boudhanath,
where the thin flagged prayers
are so threadbare it is possible
to feel Earth and Heaven coalesce,
I bought a metal soldered icon of
a little drummer boy.
Such a taut wire to tie a shoe lace
to the neat feet of Siddhartha.

I read her slim yellow volume
of voices in one sitting. She had
published them ten years before
when I was still in Boudhanath, a
tourist with bare feet. We had no
idea that our time would
come and I would somersault her
expansive gift with drumming.

The pulse of the place echoes
with ego and once again there is
an icon I fashion for myself from
fuse wire and tam-tams. I am gong
and rattle, a skin stretched across
a little drummer boy.
In her sense of scars are the beats
of Boudhanath silently at rest.

Dennis & Day's suggested reading & listening

Veronica Aaronson, *Emily's Mothers (Dempsey & Windle)*
Margaret Atwood, *The Penelopiad (Canongate)*
Gaston Bachelard, *The Poetics of Space (Penguin Classics)*
Djuna Barnes, *Nightwood (Faber & Faber)*
Basho, *Narrow Road to the Deep North and Other Travel Sketches (Penguin)*
Samuel Beckett, *Collected Poems (Faber & Faber)*
Captain Beefheart, *Trout Mask Replica (Straight)*
George Mackay Brown, *Collected Poems (Vintage Frost)*
Roberto Calasso, *The Marriage Of Cadmus And Harmony (Jonathan Cape/Vintage)*
Ítalo Calvino, *Invisible Cities (Secker & Warburg/Picador)*
Ornette Coleman, *Beauty Is A Rare Thing (Atlantic Box-Set)*
John Coltrane, *Live At The Village Vanguard, (Impulse Box-Set)*
Jayne Cortez, *Somewhere In Advance of Nowhere (High Risk)*
DakhaBrakha, *Alambari (Gargolandia)*
Miles Davis, *Tutu (Warner Bros)*
Liz Diamond, *Voices (Fore Street Press)*
Emily Dickinson, *The Complete Poems, (Faber & Faber)*
Annie Dillard, *Pilgrim At Tinker Creek (Canterbury Press)*
Bob Dylan, *Rough & Rowdy Ways (Columbia)*
John Fairfax, *Wild Children (Phoenix Press)*
Carlos Fuentes, *Terra Nostra (Secker & Warburg)*
Brian Eno, *Taking Tiger Mountain 'By Strategy' (Island)*
Allen Ginsberg, *The Lion For Real (Antilles)*
Bonnie Greer, *Langston Hughes: The Value Of Contradiction (Arcadia Books)*
Seamus Heaney, *Beowulf (Faber & Faber)*
Jimi Hendrix Experience, *Electric Ladyland (Reprise)*
Robert Hunter, *A Box of Rain (Penguin)*
Oscar Kokoschka, *A Sea Ringed With Visions (Thames & Hudson)*
Wolf Larsen, *Quiet At The Kitchen Door (download)*
Federico García Lorca, *Selected Poems (Bloodaxe Books)*
Joni Mitchell, *Mingus (A & M)*
John Moat, *Firewater And The Miraculous Mandarin (Enitharmon Press)*
Ben Okri, *The Famished Road (Jonathon Cape)*
Jennie Osborne, *Signals From The Other (Dempsey & Windle)*
Van Morrison, *Astral Weeks (Warner Bros.)*
Pauli Murray, *Song In A Weary Throat (Liveright)*
Jaques Prevert, *Trans L. Ferlinghetti, Paroles, (Penguin)*
Rainer Maria Rilke, *Selected Poems (Penguin Modern Poets)*
Jacqueline Saphra, *All My Mad Mothers (Nine Arches Press)*
Mara Adamitz Scrupe, *Beast (NFSPS Press)*
Ravi Shankar & Philip Glass, *Passages (BMG)*
Wayne Shorter, *Alegria (A & M)*
Igor Stravinsky, *City of Birmingham Symphony Orchestra, The Rite Of Spring (EMI)*
Dylan Thomas, *Collected Poems (Weidenfield & Nicolson)*
Julie Tippets & Martin Archer, *Illusion (Discus)*
Keith Tippett Octet, *Nine Dances of Patrick O' Gonogon (Discus)*
The Turbans *(Six Degrees)*
Derek Walcott, *Omeros (Faber & Faber),*
Mike Westbrook, *Glad Day - Settings of William Blake (Enja Records)*
Walt Whitman, *Leaves Of Grass (Oxford's World Classics)*
Robert Wyatt, *Rock Bottom (Virgin)*
W.B. Yeats, *Collected Poems (MacMillan)*

Acknowledgements

Publishing: Acumen magazine, *Dartmoor Dreaming;* the Guardian newspaper, the Poetry Society & Poetry Review, *Corkscrew Hill Photo* (RPD) – 1st Prize National Poetry Competition 2014; *Sestina For Christina Langrish* (SD) – shortlisted Bridport Poetry Competition 2022; all other poems are previously unpublished.

We would like to highlight the collection *Two Girls And A Beehive* by Rosie Jackson & Graham Burchell for being a significant driver in our decision to produce this duet of poems.

Roger would also like to acknowledge the important influence of his long friendship and creative interaction with the late John Moat, poet, novelist & artist. And recommend readers to all John's works at www.johnmoat.co.uk

Thanks to

Jennie Osborne, Phil Madden, Pat Fleming & Wylde Publications, Moor Poets, Diana Knight, Julian Dale, Ric White, Jon Ogborne, Christina Langrish, Graeme & Pip Harris.